JUNIOR SURVIVAL LIBRARY

## The Great White Bear

# THE POLAR BEAR

## Caroline Brett

ANGLIA
Television Limited

Boxtree

## Key to abbreviations

| | |
|---|---|
| **lb** | pound |
| **gm** | gramme |
| **kg** | kilogram |
| **in** | inch |
| **ft** | foot |
| **yd** | yard |
| **cm** | centimetre |
| **m** | metre |
| **km** | kilometre |
| **sq mile** | square mile |
| **sq km** | square kilometre |
| **kph** | kilometres per hour |
| **mph** | miles per hour |

First published in 1990 by Boxtree Limited
Copyright © 1990 Survival Anglia Limited
Text copyright © 1990 Caroline Brett

*Front jacket photographs:*
Survival Anglia/Jack Lentfer
Survival Anglia/Joel Bennett
(Polar bear and cubs on the Arctic ice pack, Alaska)
*Back jacket photograph:*
Survival Anglia/Joel Bennett
(Polar bear, 40 miles out on ice)

Line drawings by Raymond Turvey

British Library Cataloguing in Publication Data
Brett, Caroline
 The polar bear.
 1. Polar bears.
 I. Title  II. Series
 599.74446

ISBN 1-85283-069-7

Edited by Miranda Smith
Designed by Groom & Pickerill
Typeset by Rowland Phototypesetting Limited
Bury St Edmunds, Suffolk

Printed and bound in Italy
by OFSA s.p.a.

for Boxtree Limited,
36 Tavistock Street,
London WC2E 7PB

# Contents

Ice bear 4

Bear facts 6

Bear relations 8

Kingdom of the ice bear 12

Churchill bears 14

Family bear 16

Bear food 20

Bear hunt 22

Arctic animals 24

Hunters of the north 26

Bears and man 28

Glossary 30

Index 31

Acknowledgements and Notes on author 32

# Ice bear

The polar bear is often called the 'Lord of the Arctic' or 'King of the north'. Striding across the top of the world, its domain covers 13 million sq kms (5 million sq miles) of ice and snow. It is at ease in the brutal cold, the unending winter darkness, and the grinding, crushing ice.

Its true home is the Arctic pack ice which forms a cap round the North Pole. The polar bear is most frequently found at the edge of the ice cap, beside stretches of open water and where seals, its favourite prey, are plentiful.

Polar bears are excellent swimmers. They have been known to swim for hundreds of kilometres from one ice floe to another and

*The polar bear is the 'Lord of the Arctic'; the largest and strongest land carnivore.*

*Patrolling the ice. Polar bears can live to be thirty years old.*

from the coast to the pack ice. They can dive too, and stay under for as much as two minutes, although they rarely go deeper than a couple of metres. Most animals have to paddle hard to stay afloat but a polar bear can lie motionless in the water for hours. Air spaces in its fur, a waterproof coat and a thick layer of fat support it. In summer, it swims simply to cool off.

Until recently, the polar bear was thought to roam tirelessly around the Arctic, but it is now known that there are a number of main populations which live largely separate from each other. To stay at the edge of the ice – and near food – most polar bears move south in winter as the ocean freezes, and north in summer as it melts.

Polar bears live within the territories of five different nations. They are found in the United States, but only off the north and north west coasts of Alaska; in Canada; in Greenland, which is closely tied to Denmark; in the Svalbard Islands, which are governed by Norway; and in the Soviet Union.

The polar bear epitomizes life in the frozen north, yet in **evolutionary** terms, it is a relative newcomer. Between 50,000 and 100,000 years ago, a race of bears developed which could cope with life in this bleak land. In the process they underwent considerable changes. The animal we know today has become the undisputed symbol of the Arctic.

# Bear facts

Polar bears are big. They are twice the size of a lion or tiger and, when standing on their back legs, could look an elephant in the eye. The largest ever recorded weighed 1,002 kg (2,210 lb) and stood at 3.39 m (11 ft 1.5 ins). Females are smaller than males, measuring about 2 m long (6 ft 6 in) and weighing 320–410 kgs (705–904 lbs).

They are also bold. They are the only large land **carnivore** which does not instinctively fear man. In fact, they will investigate anything unfamiliar, and this, considering their size, can be highly alarming. Their reaction to a helicopter hovering overhead is to squat on their haunches and glare up or even take a swipe skywards. They are only wary of killer whales and the packs of wolves which very occasionally attack them.

The polar bear is a marvellous example of an animal totally in tune with its **environment**. A thick, winter coat and layer of fat, up to 10 cms (4 ins) thick, keeps it warm even in temperatures of minus 40°C (−72°F). They have small ears to minimise heat loss. Their creamy-white, beautifully **camouflaged** coat is also water-repellent. They lack eyelashes which would freeze in the sub-zero temperatures. Instead, they have special arctic sunglasses: a **membranous** third eyelid, like a cat's, which protects its eyes from ice glare and snow blindness.

The polar bear is surprisingly agile. Its long body and neck, narrow head, slender limbs and high rump make it look awkward, but it can run at 50 kph (35 mph), swim at 10 kph (6 mph) and leap 4.5 m (15 ft). It can travel 40 kms (25 miles) or more in a day and 1,119 kms (694 miles) during one year.

**Left** *Killer whales can be very ferocious and sometimes break through the ice to catch prey.*

**Opposite below** *The thick fur of a polar bear's paw muffles sound, which is intensified by ice.*

*The average male measures 1.6m (5ft) at the shoulder.*

## Black nose and furry paws

Against a background of ice and snow, a polar bear is almost invisible; only its black nose and small dark eyes stand out. To fool its prey, the bear peeps through half-closed lids and sometimes hides its nose with a paw.

Its paws are very large, almost a foot across, which prevents the bear sinking in soft snow. Its toes are partially webbed to make swimming easier, and the soles, apart from the pads, are completely covered with fur. This stops them freezing and helps them grip the ice. The claws, which are short, sharp and arched, act like miniature ice-picks.

# Bear relations

The polar bear's closest relative is the North American brown bear. There are several **subspecies** of brown bear distributed across Europe, northern and central Asia and North America. The grizzly, named after its 'grizzled' hair, is one kind. The Kodiak bear, which lives on Kodiak Island off Alaska, is the biggest; and the European brown bear is the smallest and the rarest. Confusingly, brown bears are not always brown. They vary from brown to black and there are even silver-grey and pale buff-coloured 'brown bears'. They all have the reputation of being dangerous but they generally flee from man. Unlike the polar bear, they are less inquisitive but more irritable, unpredictable and likely to charge, living up to their Latin name, *Ursus horribilis* ('horrible bear').

People see more American black bears than any other species because they have taken to hanging around picnic areas in the North American national parks. They **scavenge** in litter bins and beg food from tourists. Although they look friendly, they can be quite dangerous. When a visitor runs out of titbits, an impatient or hungry bear can turn nasty and should be treated with caution.

The Asiatic black bear is a different **species** from its American relative and is distinguished by a white crescent-shaped marking on its chest. It is found in southern Asia, and from there to western India, Pakistan, Afghanistan, China, Japan and Korea.

The sloth bear is also black but has a horseshoe-shaped white chest mark. It lives in the forests of eastern India and Ceylon. When

**Above** *The black bear was the original model for the teddy bear.*

**Opposite** *Two brown bears playfight. The brown bear is the polar bear's closest relative.*

the first specimen was brought back to Europe, it was thought to be related to the sloth – hence the name – because it has long, sickle-shaped claws and protruding snout, like a trunk. These special adaptations enable the bear to eat termites. Once it finds a termite

mound, it breaks through the hard outer wall with its claws and then blows the dust out with a mighty puff before sucking up the termites inside. It climbs well, shinning up trees to get at ripe fruit, flowers and wild honey.

The Malayan sun bear, which is similar to the sloth bear, is one of the world's smallest species. An adult weighs about 65 kgs (143 lbs) and a new born cub just 325 gms (11 ½ ozs). Apart from Malaya, they are also found in Kampuchea, Vietnam and Borneo.

The rarest kind of bear is the spectacled bear which once ranged across the top of South America. Today, it is only found in Peru and Ecuador because the forests where it lives have all been cut down.

**Opposite above** *The adorable lesser or red panda is shy, active at night and rarely seen in the wild.*

**Below** *A grizzly catches a salmon in an Alaskan river. Polar bears can catch fish like this.*

## The panda bear

Pandas are not true bears. They were once grouped together with the raccoons but some scientists felt that they are more closely related to American black bears. So, to avoid argument, they were put in their own separate family. There are two kinds of panda: the well-known giant panda, and the lesser or red panda.

The red panda is about the size of a small dog, has a long stripy tail and an adorable face which looks like a cross between a baby bear and a raccoon. Pandas live high in mountains, forests and bamboo thickets in China.

The giant panda is very rare. There are probably no more than one thousand left in the world. In 1975–76 large numbers starved to death when their favourite bamboo flowered and died. In 1981 the World Wide Fund for Nature (WWF) launched a major international campaign to save the giant panda.

**Left** *The spectacled bear is the world's rarest bear.*

# Kingdom of the ice bear

The high Arctic is one of the most forbidding places on earth. During the winter months, the sun never rises above the horizon and in summer it never sets. It is always bitterly cold, but the ice bear is at home in his kingdom.

Polar bears spend most of their lives walking on ice. In mid-winter, they live in a world of twilight and darkness. But they continue to hunt, relying on scent and the light reflected from the snow to guide them. They escape the worst of the winter blizzards by digging temporary shelters. Usually only pregnant females **hibernate**. But in the far north, where it gets really cold and food is hard to find in winter, all polar bears take a nap. Polar bears are not deep hibernators like chipmunks, ground squirrels and marmots that pass out completely. The body temperature of these mammals drops to just above freezing, their heartbeat falls from eighty beats a minute to barely five, and they hardly breathe. It takes them several days to drop off at the beginning of winter and as long to wake up again in spring. Although a bear's heartbeat drops from around seventy to eight beats per minute, its body temperature stays near normal and a **denning** bear can wake up in an instant. While they are in their den, the bears stop

*The ice breaks up in summer.*

*In autumn, away from the cleaning effects of snow and water, polar bear coats get dirty.*

eating and live off stored fat. They do not urinate or defecate during this time.

In the far north where the ice never melts, bears can hunt seals all year round. But further south where it is warmer, the ice pack starts to break up during the summer months. The bears swim from one pack to another to hunt seals, but eventually the ice retreats far out to sea and the bears are forced on to land.

Though polar bears are typically animals of the far north, their range encompasses some areas which lie well to the south of the Arctic circle. Hudson Bay, in Canada, is an example. Its southern shores are almost on the same **latitude** as London, yet the bay has a resident population of polar bears.

# Churchill bears

The shallow waters of Hudson Bay are a good place for ringed seals which means it is also a good place for polar bears that hunt the seals for food. But when the sea ice melts, the bears have to come ashore. They wander the coast and **tundra** just inland, eating a meagre diet of berries and vegetation. By October, they are extremely hungry and eager to start hunting again, but they must wait for the sea to freeze.

Ice first forms round sheltered bays and headlands, like Cape Churchill on the western shore of the bay. Hundreds of bears gather in the area each autumn. Out on the ice, bears usually avoid each other, except when they gather round a whale carcass. But at Cape

*At Cape Churchill, hungry bears sometimes raid the local rubbish dumps.*

*In early winter, restless shore-bound bears are eager to return to the ice to hunt seals.*

Churchill they mingle amiably, and individuals of equal size often play and wrestle together. They seem to enjoy a good romp.

South of Cape Churchill there is an important denning area where large numbers of females give birth each winter. Cubs born here rarely see much snow until they are several months old. Although the bay's coastline seems a far from typical setting for polar bears, it appears to suit them remarkably well. Triplets are raised here more frequently than elsewhere and cubs often become independent earlier than normal.

Churchill, a small town 50 kms (31 miles) west of the Cape has become famous for bears and is often called the 'polar bear capital of the world'. The rubbish dump on the outskirts of the town attracts hungry bears and they in turn attract thousands of tourists. Polar bears have become big business and the tourism brings two to three million dollars into Churchill every year.

## Bear talk

When two bears meet, they go round each other in decreasing circles, grunting and muttering, until their noses touch. The formal introduction over, they often playfight, locking jaws, rearing on their hind legs, gently pummelling, pushing and biting each other. Polar bears also hiss when annoyed and roar when wounded, but usually they are as silent as the surrounding snow.

# Family bear

Most bears spend the winter roaming the pack ice, but in autumn, the majority of pregnant females head back to land, often a small Arctic island. Here they dig a snow-den, usually in a deep drift out of the wind, in preparation for the birth of cubs. Drifting snow soon covers every trace of their activities. Some females return to the same site year after year. A passage of between 2 and 6 m (6–18 ft) long leads to a roomy inner chamber. The temperature inside stays near to freezing point, regardless of the weather outside. The bear's body heat keeps the air warm.

The cubs, usually two, less often one, and even more rarely three, are born in December or January in the den. At birth, they are rat-sized, weighing only 600–700 gms (1.5 lbs). They are also blind, deaf and totally helpless. The female cradles her tiny babies with her huge paws and breathes on them to keep them warm. The cubs grow fast on their mother's milk which tastes like cod-liver oil and is as rich as cream. At twenty-six days old, the cubs can hear but their eyes do not open for another week.

In early March when the weather warms up, the family breaks out of the den. The cubs now weigh 9–11 kgs (20–25 lbs) and are the size of a chubby fox terrier. Their mother peers outside for the first time in five months and her cubs take their first look at the big, white world.

The cubs are often reluctant to leave the safety of the den but, encouraged by their mother, it is not long before they are sliding and somersaulting in the soft snow. Despite her long winter fast, the female does not begin

*A researcher peers into a den, but the bears have deserted it.*

searching for food immediately. For a week or more she continues to use the winter den as her base. It gives the cubs the chance to accustom themselves to the outside world, and gain strength through their explorations and play.

The she-bear is now very thin and eventually, forced by hunger, she leads her babies off across the ice in search of food. As most females den on land, the family may have to trek 8–16 kms (5–10 miles) to reach the sealing grounds out at the edge of the ice. Young

*When danger threatens, the cubs stick close to their mother.*

polar bears have amazing endurance and can follow their mother for long distances, often marching behind her in line. In deep snow, they run at her side to avoid stumbling in her footprints. She stops every few hours to allow her cubs to suckle and rest.

When the female spots prey, the young stay behind until she has made a kill. In the first few days, after leaving the den, the mother

bear catches young seals. She steers clear of open water until the cubs can swim and also of dry land to avoid running into a pack of wolves which could attack her young. If the family is heavily pursued and the babies begin to tire, the female will push them on, putting her snout between their hind legs and helping them forward. Cubs in their first year are completely dependent on their mother and are unable to survive without her.

**Opposite above** *Amiable in the autumn, rival males can fight furiously in the mating season.*

**Opposite below** *Polar bears are tireless swimmers and have been seen hundreds of yards from shore.*

**Below** *Deep snowdrifts in sheltered slopes of Arctic islands are favourite denning sites.*

During their second winter, the cubs, which are now larger than an alsatian dog, den with their mother. They lose all their baby teeth, as their permanent set grows through ready for hunting in spring. After the winter rest, the cubs follow their mother once again onto the ice and learn the art of hunting by copying her every move. They are suckled until they are twenty-one months old and stay with their mother until the end of their second year, although sometimes the family holes up together for yet another winter.

Female polar bears usually mate when they are four to five years old, while males have to wait until they are at least eight. Polar bears mate during the months of April, May and June but the development of the fertilised egg is delayed, resulting in a relatively long pregnancy of 195–265 days.

# Bear food

The polar bear's chief prey are seals. Without these marine mammals, the polar bear could not survive. In spring, it hunts newborn ringed seals and, in early summer, adult bearded, harp and hooded seals which have hauled up onto the ice flows to **moult**.

Polar bears are incredibly strong and can hook a 227 kg (500 lb) seal out of the water onto the ice with a single swipe. With the bear's tremendous physical strength goes a marvellous sense of smell. It can scent a dead whale from 32 kms (20 miles) away.

Bears are very dainty eaters. They carefully skin a seal and often only eat the **blubber** lying underneath the skin, and the **entrails**. Blubber is very nutritious and fattening and a polar bear can devour 68 kgs (150 lbs) of it at a sitting. They only eat the whole carcass if they

**Opposite** *Walruses sleep and sunbathe packed close together, relying on safety in numbers.*

**Below** *Female eider ducks are well camouflaged but a bear can discover a nest and eat the eggs.*

are very hungry. Polar bears are also surprisingly clean. After feeding, they carefully lick their fur and give their face a wipe with their paws, like a cat.

When there are no seals to hunt in midsummer the bears become **omnivorous**. They will eat almost anything they can find. They patrol the bottoms of bird-nesting cliffs looking for eggs and chicks that have fallen off the ledges. They search for eider duck nests on the ground, scavenge along the shoreline and even raid tents and camps for food. During lemming plagues, the bears stuff themselves with these small rodents. In summer they eat bilberries, **crowberries** and cranberries as well as grasses and seaweed.

Some polar bears have a special technique for hunting ducks. They swim slowly towards a flock, scarcely rippling the surface with only their head showing above the water. As the ducks dive for safety, so does the bear, catching one underwater.

Polar bears treat walruses with respect, because they are three times the bear's size and armed with long, sharp tusks. However, the bears do sometimes kill an unguarded calf.

# Bear hunt

*Some Arctic foxes 'adopt' polar bears following them all winter long and eating their left-overs.*

## Constant companion

The Arctic fox is the polar bear's **scavenger**. When a bear kills a seal, it normally only eats the blubber, giving seabirds and foxes an opportunity to scavenge the leavings. During the winter months many Arctic foxes follow the bears far out onto the ice and rely on their hunting exclusively for their food.

A hunting bear moves silently across the snow with its head low. It searches most intensely in areas of open water, near glacier mouths and icebergs. When it spots a sleeping seal it zigzags forward using any hummock or chunk of ice as cover. Out in the open, it flattens itself like a rug with its neck and snout on the ice. Pushing with its hind legs, it moves slowly forward, stopping dead if the seal lifts its head. When it is a few feet away, it swiftly kills its **prey** with a single stroke.

Sometimes a bear will slip silently into the water, hind legs first. Looking like a floating block of ice, it drifts towards its prey. Several feet from the seal, it sinks below the surface and then, at the last minute, springs out of the water onto its unsuspecting prey. Another tactic is to wait patiently, sometimes for hours, at a seal's breathing hole. When the seal appears, the bear bangs its victim's head against the ice, killing it instantly. When seals are plentiful, a bear normally kills one every few days.

Some seals bear their young in dens which are covered by several metres of snow. Although the den is not visible from above, the bear can detect the seal by smell. Scraping away the hard, frozen outer layer of ice, the bear then raises itself on its hind legs and drops the full weight of its body onto the remaining snow. The force of the pouncing bear collapses the roof of the seal's den, and the bear can reach its prey.

**Opposite** *A polar bear's superb sense of smell guides it over great distances to food.*

# Arctic animals

Arctic animals have several characteristics which help them survive in their cold hostile environment. Polar bears, Arctic foxes and hares, snowy owls and some **gyrfalcons** are white all year round; other animals like weasels, ptarmigan and some lemmings turn white for camouflage in winter. They are generally larger than their southern counterparts.

*Although musk-ox resemble cattle, they are probably more closely related to sheep and goats.*

A large body has a smaller surface area through which to lose heat.

Some fish have **antifreeze** in their blood which enables them to survive in the icy sea. Certain seals have **arteries** and **veins** in their flippers which lie next to each other, speeding up blood flow and keeping their limbs warm.

The musk-ox has a dense woolly undercoat which protects the animal from the cold and damp, and a shaggy, dark brown mantle of long outer guard hairs, reaching almost to the

**Above** *Reindeer and caribou are strong swimmers and cross many rivers on their search for food.*

**Below** *Snowy owl chicks are covered in dense down to protect them from the perishing cold.*

ground in winter. Protected by this immense coat it can withstand the worst Arctic weather.

Arctic plants too are specially adapted. Like the musk-ox many of them are very hairy. The long fibres trap an insulating layer of air which helps keep the plant warm. They grow low to the ground to avoid the howling wind and complete their life cycle in a very short time – the Arctic poppy grows, flowers and sets seed in only fifteen days.

## The remarkable reindeer

Reindeer are one of the most remarkable animals living in the Arctic. They have a thick, waterproof coat which keeps them warm even in a blizzard. A reindeer fur jacket makes a good life jacket because the hair is hollow and filled with air which makes it **buoyant**. Reindeer can find and dig up food in what seems a barren wasteland. Their **splayed** hooves have a sharp edge which can cut through all but the hardest ice. Their chief food is lichen, often called reindeer moss.

# Hunters of the north

Eskimos have lived with polar bears for thousands of years. They fear them but also worship them as gods. They believe they are beasts of infinite wisdom that can communicate with the spirits, and if an old person is killed by a polar bear, their soul will be rekindled and come alive again. To absorb the magic powers of the bear, many Inuit Eskimos wore a bear tooth pendant.

There are many Eskimo stories about polar bears. In Alaska, they say there is a ten-legged bear which few hunters have looked at and lived to tell the tale! In Hudson Bay, there is a legendary giant polar bear which lives at the bottom of the sea. When a whaling captain dropped a depth charge to kill it, the bear almost capsized his ship.

Eskimos kill bears for their fur and meat but they believe that, in death, a bear's spirit is

**Opposite** *Eskimos probably learned how to hunt seals by copying the polar bear.*

**Below** *The Eskimos call the polar bear 'the ever-wandering one'. They use their skins for clothing and as rugs.*

released. They treat polar bears with great respect. No Eskimo hunter will ridicule, belittle or make jokes about a polar bear because to do so will bring bad luck. Polar bears, they say, are as smart as humans.

Bear skins are highly prized. Polar Eskimos still wear mittens, boots, shoes and trousers made of bear hide; the latter must be the most expensive trousers in the world. The Eskimos use bear rugs to sit and sleep on. Even small pieces are valued: the grease from the fur is used to oil sledge runners – apparently no substitute works as well. Bear-hide overboots, fur side down, are worn to muffle the sound of footsteps during a seal hunt. Eskimos also use a bearskin shield, which looks like an umbrella, for stalking seals out on the ice.

Some Eskimos will only feed bear meat to their dogs. In other tribes, bear stew is popular but it has to be well cooked because there are **parasites** in under-cooked flesh. Also the liver of a polar bear contains so much vitamin A it can lead to vitamin poisoning.

# Bears and man

*A polar bear research programme in Alaska includes tagging and marking bears.*

Polar bears have fascinated man since the time of the Pharaohs. Drawings in one Egyptian tomb show details of a burial chamber for a polar bear. The bears' dignity, majesty and rarity made them coveted mascots in the courts of kings and emperors.

Early explorers and whalers hunted polar bears for their skins and meat. In Europe the thick, white pelts were sought after for rugs. They were also highly prized for altars, and pulpits where priests used them to keep their feet warm.

As more people ventured into the Arctic, the polar bear's awesome reputation grew. Their habit of approaching out of curiosity led men to believe that they were about to attack. Polar bears can be dangerous but they do not normally attack man. Those which have done have usually been sick or starving, or the victim reeked of seal meat and the bears mistook them for their natural prey.

Where food is concerned, polar bears are far from retiring. Not long ago, a crew from a Canadian Coast Guard ship amused themselves by tossing a young male some molasses, jam, salt beef, salami, chocolate and a jar of peanut butter. Not surprisingly, the bear stuck his head through a porthole asking for more. At a sister ship, after being thrown a steak, the bear climbed aboard, to the dismay of the crew. When the crew turned the hoses on him, the bear loved it and raised his forelegs to get the stream under its armpits! Only a rocket, fired next to him, moved him off.

Human invasion of the Arctic has greatly reduced the polar bear populations. Today there are only between 20,000 and 40,000 spread across the top of the globe. In 1965 every nation which borders the Arctic attended a polar bear conference. They unanimously agreed to declare the polar bear of international importance and to ban hunting of any female with young.

Though over-hunting is largely a thing of the past, polar bears now face a greater threat. Petroleum exploration and development is firmly established in the Arctic. Oil spills kill seals and in turn the bears that rely on them for food. Conservation is of international concern and, thanks to all the nations involved, polar bear populations are now stable, while some are even on the increase. The polar bear symbolises the spirit of one of the last great unspoilt wildernesses on earth. Long may it continue to reign supreme in its icebound home.

*As the Arctic continues to be explored by man, the polar bear's future is uncertain.*

# GLOSSARY

**Antifreeze** A substance which stops water from turning to ice at 0°C.

**Arteries** Tubes that carry blood rich in oxygen away from the heart.

**Blubber** The fat found under the skin of marine mammals.

**Buoyant** Having a tendency to float.

**Camouflage** The ability an animal has to hide by blending in with its background.

**Carnivore** An animal which eats meat.

**Crowberry** An Arctic berry, similar to a cranberry.

**Denning** Hibernating or having cubs in a den.

**Entrails** The internal organs of an animal.

**Environment** The natural surrounding of an animal or plant.

**Evolution** The slow process by which animals adapt, over many generations, to their environment.

**Gyrfalcon** A large falcon of the northern regions.

**Hibernate** To be inactive or sleep during the cold winter months.

**Latitude** The lines drawn on maps of the world which run horizontally round the earth at intervals above and below the equator.

**Membranous** With a thin, pliable layer of tissue.

**Moult** to shed fur which is replaced by new growth.

**Omnivorous** Eating both vegetable and animal matter.

**Parasite** An organism that grows, feeds and shelters on a different organism.

**Prey** An animal which is hunted and eaten by another animal.

**Scavenge** To feed on leftovers or dead bodies of other animals.

**Splayed** Spread out or apart.

**Species** A type of animal (or plant) that can interbreed successfully with others of its kind, but not with those of a different type.

**Sub-species** Sub-division of species (**see Species**).

**Tundra** A treeless Arctic region where the soil just below ground level is frozen throughout the year.

**Veins** Tubes which carry blood to the heart.

# Index

The entries in **bold** are illustrations.

Alaska 26
antifreeze 24, 30
Arctic foxes 22, **22**, 24
Arctic hares 24

bears
   American black bear 8, **8**
   Asiatic black bear 8
   European 8
   grizzly 8, **10**
   Kodiak 8
   Malayan sun bear 10
   North American brown 8, **9**
   sloth bear 8
   spectacled bear 10, **11**
breathing holes 22

camouflage 7, **20** 24, 30
Canadian Coast Guard 28
conservation 29
cubs 14, 15, 16, **17**, 19

denning, 12–13, 16, **16**, 17, 19, 22, 30
ducks **20**, 21

Eskimos 26–7, **26**
evolution 30

fighting **18**
fishing **10**

gyrfalcons 24, 30

habitat 4–5, 6
   Arctic 4, 5, 12–13, 16, 24–5, 28–9
hibernation 12–13, 30
Hudson Bay 13, 14, 26
   Cape Churchill 14–15, **14**
   tourism 15
hunting 5, 13, **15**, 22–3, 26, 27, **27**, 28

ice cap 4

killer whales 6, **6**

lemmings 21, 24

migration 5
moulting 20, 30
musk-oxen 24–5, **24**

North Pole 4

over-hunting 29

pack ice 5
panda bears 11
   giant 11
   red 11, **11**
paws 7, **7**
Pharaohs 28
plants 25
   Arctic poppy 25
playfighting 15, **9**

polar bears
   agility 6
   as gods 26
   coat 5, 6, **13**, 26
   heartbeats 12
   in legend 26
   sense of smell 20, **23**
   size **4**, 6, **7**
   strength 20
   third eyelid 6
   weight **4**, 6
prey 23, 28, 30

reindeer 25, **25**
   hooves 25
reindeer moss 25

scavenging **14**, 22, 30
seals 5, 13, 14, 19, 20–1, 22, 24
   dens 22
snowy owls **25**
swimming 4, 5, **18**

tagging **28**
teeth pendants 26

walruses 21, **21**
weasels 24
whales 14
wolves 6, 19
World Wide Fund for Nature (WWF) 11

## Picture Acknowledgements

The publishers would like to thank the
Survival Anglia picture library
and the following photographers for the use
of photographs on the pages listed:

Jack Lentfer 4, 17, 18 (bottom), 27; Joel Bennett 5, 7 (top and bottom), 12, 13, 14, 16, 18 (top), 19, 21, 24, 25 (top), 26, 28, 29; Jeff Foott 6, 10, 11 (top); Claude Steelman 6; Liz Bomford 11 (bottom); Jen and Des Bartlett 15; Cindy Boxton 20; Caroline Brett 22; Tony and Liz Bomford 25 (bottom).

## About the author

Caroline Brett has a B.Sc Hons degree in Zoology from Bristol University. After travelling through North, Central and South America she joined Radio Avonside (now Great Western Radio). Caroline now works for Survival Anglia as a writer and producer of natural history documentaries for the long-running Survival series and has also made programmes for Anglia Television's children's series ANIMALS IN ACTION. She is the author of *The Lion* in the Junior Survival Library.

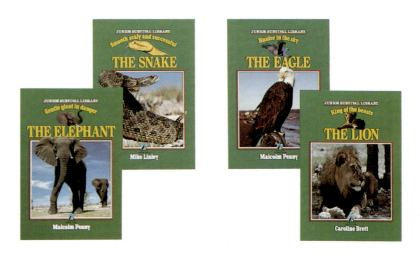

**The first four titles in the Junior Survival Library.**